Uchenna Egbuchulam

AuthorHouse™ UK Ltd.
1663 Liberty Drive
Bloomington, IN 47403 USA
www.authorhouse.co.uk
Phone: 0800.197.4150

© 2014 Uchenna Egbuchulam. All rights reserved.

No part of this book may be reproduced, stored in a retrieval system, or transmitted by any means without the written permission of the author.

Published by AuthorHouse 09/23/2014

ISBN: 978-1-4969-9206-2 (sc)
ISBN: 978-1-4969-9205-5 (hc)
ISBN: 978-1-4969-9207-9 (e)

Any people depicted in stock imagery provided by Thinkstock are models, and such images are being used for illustrative purposes only. Certain stock imagery © Thinkstock.

This book is printed on acid-free paper.

Because of the dynamic nature of the Internet, any web addresses or links contained in this book may have changed since publication and may no longer be valid. The views expressed in this work are solely those of the author and do not necessarily reflect the views of the publisher, and the publisher hereby disclaims any responsibility for them.

Scripture quotations marked NKJV are taken from the New King James Version. Copyright © 1982 by Thomas Nelson, Inc. Used by permission. All rights reserved.

Scripture quotations marked NIV are taken from the Holy Bible, New International Version® NIV®. Copyright © 1973, 1978, 1984 by International Bible Society. Used by permission of Zondervan. All rights reserved. [Biblica]

Scripture quotations marked KJV are from the Holy Bible, King James Version (Authorized Version). First published in 1611. Quoted from the KJV Classic Reference Bible, Copyright © 1983 by The Zondervan Corporation.

Unless otherwise indicated, all scripture quotations are from The Holy Bible, English Standard Version® (ESV®). Copyright ©2001 by Crossway Bibles, a division of Good News Publishers. Used by permission. All rights reserved.

To the Almighty God and to all evangelists, pastors, and ministers of the gospel.

Contents

Acknowledgement ix
Foreword xv
Preface xvii
Who Is a Youth? 1
Peer Group Influence 7
Alcohol Consumption 13
Smoking 19
Sexual Immorality 21
Chasing after Wealth 31
God's Expectation for Youths 36
Reward for Holding on to Christ 51
Turning impossibility to possibility 61
Seeds of Self-Fulfilment 77
Final Word 84
Prayer for Salvation 86

References 87

Acknowledgement

I thank the cosmic, the Creator of the entire universe, and everything that has breath for the inspiration to write this book and the finances to publish it.

I glorify his name for the lives of my parents, Hon. Dr. and Mrs. C. J. Egbuchulam, for their parental support and care and for making the right decision to send me to study in Ukraine. Their love has been my driving force to academic success so far.

I must also seize this opportunity to thank my uncle Dr. Osmond Ukanacho, thanks for the pep talk you gave me before I came to Ukraine and for being supportive of me, you assist me whenever I'm in need without thinking twice. May the good Lord continue to bless you.

I thank my siblings Obinna, Okenna, Gozie, Nneka, and Chiamaka for their love and support and for keeping me abreast with news from home and about their personal lives.

To other extended members of my family, I also say thanks.

I thank God for the fellowship of Christian students in Ternopil for being my family in Ukraine. Special thanks go to Dr. Elas Ekiyor, the first person in Ukraine to give me a revelation of God's purpose for my life and to help me work in line with it.

I appreciate you, Dr. Eso Christopher Akinleye, for being so interested in my spiritual growth and development and for teaching me the Word whenever you could. I appreciate you, also, a great deal, Dr. Emmanuel Nnamani, my friend, my brother, and my predecessor as evangelism coordinator of Fellowship of Christian Students Ukraine. Without you, I wouldn't have joined the evangelism team, and I wouldn't have learnt all I learnt from you.

I also appreciate the general coordinator of this unique fellowship, Minister Aliu Pelumi. I lack words to describe how much value and impact your friendship has made in my life. Thank you for your academic support and for pushing me to succeed, even in ministry. I remember when I was called to be the evangelism coordinator. I said I couldn't do it, and you said, "God wouldn't call you if he wasn't sure you could function in that capacity."

Thank you, Dr. Noble Ngaobiwu, for being a friend and a brother and for helping me get settled in Ukraine.

I extend my thanks to the leaders of FCS, whom I have worked with and whom I have come to love and admire for believing in me. Praise, Ayo, Pelumi, Samuel, Elochukwu, Oluchi, Titi, Debbie, David, Ekemini, and Kelvin.

More acknowledgements go to the members of the evangelism department of FCS: Amba, Ayo, Molly, Samuel, Adaeze, Eloho, and Watter for having faith in me as their spiritual leader, even when I didn't have faith in myself.

I thank other ministers of the gospel who have touched my life from a distance: Pastor Chris Oyakilome, Pastor Creflo Dollar, Pastor Joel Osteen, Bishop T. D. Jakes, and Pastor Joseph Prince. I listen to your messages a lot, and they have inspired me in innumerable ways.

I also celebrate Minister Odiah and Minister Chioma Okeke, close friends whom I have also learnt from here in Ternopil. May the Lord bless you.

I must thank my group mates Daniel, Chuba, Frederick, Ifeanyi, Franklyn, and Amba for accepting me as one of them when I was transferred from my previous group. We have had fun together, and we have shared experiences. Their constant arguments on how most students behave here inspired me the more to write this book.

Lastly, special thanks to my dear friend, Stephanie Mbanaso. You have always had faith in me. You have always cared about my welfare. Thanks a lot for helping me make inquiries about publishing.

People advertise their products and skills. Almost anything can be done or manufactured. But Jesus Christ is totally unique. He offers what no founder of any religion offers or can offer. The God of the Bible says, "Look, I am making everything new!" Rev. 21:5 NLT If we allow him, he will take our broken and sinful lives and turn them into his dwelling place. All his beginnings are new, creative, and sparkling. He is the God of new life, new wine, new songs, new treasures, the new man, a new covenant, a new commandment, a new and living way, and a new kingdom. We are new creatures in Christ Jesus. Reach out to him now, and ask him to forgive your sins and save you. He will surely do it. God bless you.

Evangelist Reinhard Bonnke

Foreword

Many live with vital, unanswered questions all their lives, but with this book, you do not have to live in the dark anymore. How can I live right? How can my heart be renewed? You will find the answers within the pages of this life-transforming book.

It's my wish that youths today would get hold of this book. I pray that every undergraduate will start out with lessons from this great book. We are the leaders of today (every tomorrow eventually becomes a today), and we cannot deliver to our world greater than we have in our heart. Esau sought a change of mind with tears but could not obtain one. Here is a timely opportunity for God to restructure your mind and remove what is in your mind that poisons everything else.

Gird Your Mind is an easy read for all to comprehend. The writer, Uche, has done an amazing work, buttressing each message with the intention of easy comprehension. This book should be a must read for everyone, cutting across all age groups but mostly focused on the youths.

Thank you, Uche. You are always delivering, and a great future awaits you. I appreciate the privilege given me to write the foreword of this life-transforming book. I am proud of you, but much more important is that God is proud of you and still will be in many more to come.

Yours in the Lord,

Aliu Oluwapelumi, general coordinator, Fellowship of Christian Students

Ternopil, Ukraine

Preface

I bring you greetings in the name of God the father, the Son, and the Holy Ghost, who has empowered me to bear witness of his perfect love for mankind. His unique love has been shed abroad for all, but not everyone has come to a realization and understanding of this. I was actually studying for my physiology class and humming a spiritual song by Pastor Chris Oyakilome, in the early hours of one morning, when the Lord laid it down in my heart to write this book. He said, "Son, you have been saved. You pray and sing in the Holy Ghost, and as a result, you are enjoying spiritual, financial, and academic grace. But there are youths like you out there who are not." And then he reminded me of the scripture that says, "Don't let the excitement of youth cause you to forget your creator. Honour him in your youth before you grow old and say, "life is not pleasant anymore." Ecclesiastes 12:1 NLT

Every day we live, we grow one day older. Some old people wish they were younger so they could correct some of the mistakes they made as youths. The right foundation that determines how we end up is set in our youth. The friends we keep and the activities we are involved in can tell much about us from a distance. Growing older is not something we have control over, but how we choose to live each day is something we do have control over. God desires that we learn to age with grace and dignity, and that's why he laid emphasis on the importance of remembering him in the days of our youth.

The Lord said to Moses, "Take Joshua son of Nun, a man in whom is the spirit and lay your hand on him. Make him stand before Eleazar the priest and all the congregation, and you shall commission him in their sight. You shall invest him with some of your authority, that all the congregation of the children of Israel may obey him" (Numbers 27: 18–20).

Many young men among the Israelites were about the same age as Joshua, son of Nun, but no doubt, he was different from the rest of them. So different was he that Moses chose him to be next in command. What made Joshua different was his love for God. Joshua knew the importance of walking with God and being in his presence. The Bible tells us that, after Moses departed from the tabernacle,

Joshua remained (Exodus 33: 11). He understood that there was so much to gain from being in God's presence.

God is looking for young men and women like Joshua whom he can fill with his spirit and whom he can empower to do exploits for the kingdom of God.

I read a story about a man who had rushed up to a ferry he needed to catch to get across a lake. He arrived breathless after running full steam to get there, but the gateman shut the door in his face; he just missed the boat. A bystander remarked to him, "I guess you didn't run fast enough!"

The disappointed man answered, "I ran fast enough, but I didn't start on time." To accomplish the most for God in a lifetime, you must start early: "In the days of thy youth." Ecclesiastes 12:1

The wisest man who has ever lived stated in Proverbs 22: 6 that we should "Train up a child in the way he should go so that when he is old, he will not depart from it."

In this book, the Lord will teach you the importance of being rooted in him in the days of thy youth, how to set the right foundation, and how to be productive. Be blessed as you read.

Evangelist Uche Egbuchulam
Fellowship of Christian students, Ternopil, Ukraine

Who Is a Youth?

Wikipedia defines youth as the time of life that is neither childhood nor adulthood but rather somewhere in between. The most difficult time in life is our youth – a time in which we are hardly old enough to be on our own, yet we feel a sense of independence, perhaps because we have begun university and are away from the prying eyes of our parents. Youths are constantly trying to discover themselves, and that's why they dress weird, act weird, and sometimes speak without weighing their words. The journey to self-discovery is difficult if we fail to trust in the Lord or acknowledge his existence.

The Bible says "The imagination of man's heart is evil from his youth" (Genesis 8: 2 KJV). The Apostle Paul advised Timothy to flee from youthful lusts, 2 timothy 2:22 but God also recognizes the value of youth. Youths are full of life and full of ambitions, visions, and goals. That's why he wants us to make the right choices.

First Timothy 2: 3–4 says, "For this is good and acceptable in the sight of God our savior who will have all men to be saved and to come unto the knowledge of truth" (KJV).

God wants to deliver you from sin, from the devil's captivity. He wants to deliver you from futility, vanity, and a wasted lifestyle.

The first thing God wants youth to discover is their purpose on earth, the reason for their existence. The Bible tells us, "To everything there is a season and a time to every purpose under the Heaven" (Ecclesiastes 3: 1 KJV). There is a purpose attached to everything that God makes; God does not create anything without purpose. The Bible pointed out that the thoughts he has for us are thoughts of good and not of evil, to give us an expected end. If you can find God's purpose for your life and walk in that purpose, the devil can do nothing against you. Everything that happens to you from the time you discover your purpose will be for your good.

Have you ever paused to consider why God has placed you where you are presently or what he wants from you? Joseph, at the age of seventeen, discovered the purpose of God for his life and shared the revelation with his brothers. They thought they could destroy him, but because he already had the right stand in God, everything they did to him negatively, from that point, became a step in the fulfilment of the purpose he had discovered.

King David, as a youth, deeply trusted in God's ability to deliver him from whatever harm came his way. He demonstrated that several times: when he rescued his father's flocks from wild beasts and when he became Israel's saviour, defeating a philistine who was many times his height and who could have easily squeezed the life out of him if he had leaned unto his own mortal strength and understanding. That mindset of trusting God was what led him to become Israel's king, after Saul.

The Bible also made mention of Josiah, who ascended the throne of Israel at eight. "And like unto him was there no king before him, that turned to the Lord with all his heart, and with all his soul, and with all his might, according to all the law of Moses; neither after him arose there any like him." (2 Kings 23: 25 KJV).

He loved the Lord so much that he made sure there were no idol worshippers in his kingdom, and the lord made his reign successful.

Daniel, Shadrach, Meshach, and Abednego, even in captivity, still held on to their faith and trusted the Lord, which led to their promotion above the wise men of Babylon.

We also read about Joshua, who loved God and obeyed all his commandments. He was Moses's disciple, or apprentice, who took over at the death of Moses and led Israel into the Promised Land.

How about Samuel, who was dedicated to the Lord from his birth? He diligently served the Lord under Eli the priest and obeyed the Lord. The Bible told us the Lord revealed to Samuel that he had rejected Eli and chosen him to serve in his place. What if Samuel had been like Eli and his sons? His destiny would have been rewritten.

Mary, the mother of Jesus Christ, took a right stand by making a decision to remain a virgin until she was ready for marriage, and she found favour in the sight of God.

Still today, the Roman Catholics honour her. Imagine what would have happened if God hadn't found a virgin to bring forth Christ; perhaps no one would have salvation today.

I cannot overemphasize the importance of serving God in youth. Youths today think serving God is overrated. They want to have all the fun in the world, and then later, when they have grown older, they start asking for God's mercy. Trust me; they can't deceive God. The Lord knows it is difficult to serve him now because of the numerous challenges and temptations youths encounter. But he insists on them serving him in the days of their youth, for it is in their youth that they decide how they end up. Rely on his grace.

The Bible says, "My people are destroyed for lack of knowledge." The Lord will be upset if we fail, because we have knowledge of what he wants us to do and that is to serve him in our youth. Proverbs 19: 20 (KJV) says to "Hear counsel, and receive instruction, that thou mayest be wise in thy latter end."

Serving God is the best investment you can make; it pays in every area of your life. God's purpose will always prevail above your priorities if you give him the opportunity.

Subsequent chapters outline the factors that prevent youths from serving the Lord, and we will see how to overcome them.

Peer Group Influence

According to Wikipedia, A peer group is both a social group and a primary group of people who have similar interests (homophily), age, background, and social status. The members of this group are likely to influence the person's beliefs and behaviour. Peer groups contain hierarchies and distinct patterns of behavior. 18 year olds are not in a peer group with 14 year olds even though they may be in school together.

As a toddler or a child in preschool, it is solely the responsibility of your parents to hook you up with people of the same age group perhaps children of their friends or coworkers; you play with them and interact with them. As you progress further perhaps in your middle childhood from the ages of ten onwards, you tend to choose your friends among people you are attracted to or people with the same interest. This period of development is one in which the child is directed away from the family group and is centered on the wider world of peer relationships. A connection is established between the child and his/

her peers. One in which they tend to influence each other's decisions.

This also continues in later childhood (adolescence period to youth). Peer group can be of positive or negative influence.

For instance if you are in the midst of friends who are serious minded, studious and have positive visions, goals, or aspirations, one way or the other you will be influenced to start reasoning alike. Proverbs 27:17 "Iron sharpens iron, and so one man sharpens another". ESV

Among friends you have this sense of belonging especially if they are friends you can count on to protect your interests. You are relaxed knowing fully well that they have got your back. They can make excuses for you or defend you.

Friends can offer positive advice or give you the courage to do certain things. I remember once in high school, my friends advised me to sign up for an essay competition, even though I didn't win because there were better writers but it gave me the opportunity to learn new words and improve myself.

On one occasion in high school, I met this pretty girl I liked and wanted to get to know but I was a bit shy, I talked to my friends and they encouraged me to approach her. It turned out she was friendly and that she liked the same movies and she read the same books that I read so we became friends. This scenario is not really applicable in this context but I am sure I made a point.

Also in high school I remember when we were making the decision to be in the science or art class, a friend of mine approached me and asked if he could join me in the science class or if he should be in the art class, I told him being in the science class was worth a try and it wouldn't be too difficult if he will learn to study and avoid distractions, he took my advice and of recent he just graduated from a federal university in Nigeria where he studied biochemistry.

Basically good friends encourage each other and can be of positive influence to one another.

Your peers can also make you do the wrong things. The Bible said, "Be not deceived: evil communications corrupts good manners" (1 Corinthians 15: 33 KJV).

Often times, youths give in to the negative influence of peer pressure because they don't want society to reject them. When they give in to peer pressure, they become like mindless robots, because they allow other people to control them.

When faced with peer pressure to do the wrong thing, try the following:

Weigh the consequences. Ask yourself, what if I get into trouble doing this? What will my parents think of me? Galatians 6: 7 (KJV) says, "Be not deceived; God is not mocked: for whatsoever a man soweth, that shall he also reap."

Maintain a good conscience and look beyond the present. Certain mistakes are irreversible. Some students in one of the schools I attended got drunk and still drove. They got involved in a car accident and lost their lives, and that was how their dreams ended. Your friends might call you names and despise you, but don't let them break your spirit. The same people will always come back to seek help from you.

Learn to say no when being lured to do the wrong thing. This reminds me of a song my high school principal taught us: "When by others urged to tread a path you should not go, let them blame you if they will but firmly answer no. Do the right with all your might, a pure example show. Don't fail to speak the little word, 'No, No, No.'" This song came back into my mind when I discovered God's purpose for my life. I usually remember it when situations want to lure me to go contrary to the Word of God. The book of Titus, chapter 2, verse 12 (NIV), also laid emphasis on the word no. It teaches us to say no to ungodliness and worldly passions and to live self-controlled, upright, and godly lives in this present age.

In summary, peer group influence is a good thing if it will lead you to fulfil God's purpose for your life but, if not, learn to say no. It's not always easy to resist negative peer pressure, but when you do, it is easy to feel good about it afterwards. And you may even be a positive influence on your peers who feel the same way – often it just takes one person to speak out or take a different action to change a situation. Your friends may follow if you have the courage to do something different or refuse to go along with the group. Consider yourself a leader, and know that you have the potential to make a difference.

In the next chapter, we will look at some negative things your peers may lead you to do and how to resist them or stop doing them if you already are.

Alcohol Consumption

Personally, I don't have a problem with alcohol if consumed moderately and indoors, but it becomes a very big problem if youths abuse it, as so many do today. Alcohol abuse leads to addiction, and when one develops a daily habit of consuming alcohol, it leads to a destructive pattern of alcohol use that includes spending money to buy it regularly, even when one is aware of the detrimental effects it has on life.

Alcohol affects a teen's brain differently than it does an adult's. Teens' brains are still growing and developing in ways that shape their perceptions of emotions, excitement, danger, and some memories. Heavy alcohol use during this time of brain development could lead to permanent changes.

Alcohol offers a fast way out of your immediate stress or problem and helps you fit in and feel good. But alcohol impairs judgment, a big problem for youths who already lack experience, and alcohol intoxication can be fatal. The negative effects include:

- Alcoholism. People who begin drinking before age 15 are four times more likely to become alcohol-dependent than those who wait until 21.

- Fatal accidents. Alcohol is to be blamed for many drownings and traffic deaths involving teens. Excessive alcohol causes one to lose control of the frontal region of the brain that is involved in learning, impulse control, planning, decision-making, and voluntary motor movement. As a result, accidents occur while driving.

- Violence. Underage drinkers are more likely to commit or be victims of violent crimes.

- Sexual activity. Adolescents who use alcohol are more likely to be sexually active at an earlier age and have unprotected sex.

- Suicide. Teen drinking has been linked with contemplating or committing suicide.

- School performance. High school students who drink are more likely to drop out of school and disdain good grades. Heavy drinking hampers brain development, memory, and learning ability.

- Health damage. Anyone who drinks a lot faces heart and central nervous system damage, cirrhosis and cancer of the liver, stroke, and risk for overdose.

- Drinking in excess can lead to the use of other drugs like marijuana, cocaine, or heroine

How does one start consuming alcohol?

Alcohol consumption is a result of several environmental, psychological, and genetic factors. Some youths consume alcohol, smoke cigarettes, or do drugs because they saw their parents, older siblings, or friends doing so.

I was born into a family that entertained visitors on a regular basis because of my dad's political affiliations. Alcohol was always available. I started drinking at a young age because I saw my friends and some other people drink. My mum caught me on one occasion and gave me the scolding of my life. Still, regular exposure to friends and people who drank caused me to develop a tolerance for alcohol to the extent that I could consume five bottles of beer, a bottle of champagne or any wine, an average sized bottle of cognac, or any spirit and still be in control of myself. It's nothing to be proud of; so many youths are like that presently. It was sheer alcohol abuse, and if I had continued like that, I would have had serious health issues by now. In my own case, the Lord was able to save me through the Word of God. A pastor friend of mine, Pastor Daniel Rhema, said something that made serious sense to me and gave me cause to ponder and deliberate. He said, "If the devil wants to destroy a man who is destined to be great, he gives him an insatiable appetite and love for alcohol with the intention of destroying his liver and shortening his life span."

I went home that day, meditated on what I had heard, and asked the Lord to cause me to stop drinking. It took some time because I seriously loved alcohol, but it became a reality. I rarely take alcohol now.

Alcohol drives youths far away from God. The devil has a way of planting the urge to drink alcohol in the mind of youths on a Saturday night so that they could develop a hangover on Sunday and not be in church to worship God.

Beware of the devices of the devil, for the devil will try any means to keep you far from God. And being far from God means you don't get close enough to discover your purpose. If it happens that you die prematurely in a car accident because of excessive alcohol, that becomes your end.

Les Brown must have considered all these when he said this quote, "The grave yard is the richest place on earth, because it is here that you will find all the hopes and dreams that were never fulfilled, the books that were never written, the songs that were never sung, the inventions that were never shared, the cures that were never discovered, all because someone was too afraid to take that first step, keep with the problem, or determined to carry out their dream."

"One of the greatest tragedies in life is to watch potential die untapped." Myles Munroe.

It is in our youth that the Lord implants dreams and imbeds potentials in us, but we never discover them because we are far from him and too busy indulging in irrelevant things.

"Wine is a mocker and beer a brawler; whoever is led astray by them is not wise" (Proverbs 20: 1 NIV).

In conclusion, alcohol consumed in moderate quantities is neither harmful nor addictive. Doctors even advise people to take a little alcohol for their heart; however, drunkenness is a sin. One can easily be tempted to take alcohol in excess; therefore, it is best for every Christian to abstain from drinking alcohol. There is still hope for many youths who are addicted to alcohol consumption because of the unnecessary desire to live up to societal standards or to maintain friendships with peers. Alcohol use does more harm than good. You can start by reducing your intake and then asking the Lord to help you stop completely, and he will.

Smoking

A lot of people in society today smoke. It's a wrong decision for one to smoke because of the health risks. Many of us are aware of these health risks, yet we choose to ignore the warnings from health experts.

Youths today inhale a lot of substances in the name of smoking: cigarette tobacco, marijuana, and of recent, shisha. They are all addictive, and once they start smoking, it's very difficult to stop. It all starts from being in the midst of friends or people who smoke. They are tempted to try one stick and then another and yet another. They go home and smoke another. Before they know it, it becomes a daily routine and they get hooked.

I did try smoking occasionally when I found myself among friends who smoked, especially when we went clubbing. It's a mystery I didn't get hooked.

The grace on everyone's life is different. You might not get as lucky as I did, so it's best you discipline yourself and don't start at all. I'm considering the health risks. Now I'm writing as a medical student and not establishing if it's a sin or not.

Don't shorten your lifespan by smoking; it's not God's will for anyone to do so.

What if you were created to do something at a particular age and you don't live up to that age simply because you just couldn't quit smoking.

Self-admonition is the best form of discipline. Don't carry your inventions to the graveside.

"Whoever heeds instruction is on the path to life, but he who rejects reproof leads others astray" (Proverbs 10: 17 ESV).

Sexual Immorality

This is one sin most youths indulge in on a regular basis. The mentality youths have is that as soon as you find one who you are attracted to and who has accepted to date you, the next thing should be to go ahead and have sex. some guys wouldn't even want to be with a girl if she refuses to have sex with him, on the other hand some girls would want a guy to have sex with them just to see how sexually active he is and how long he could last in the act.

Some others address themselves as "friends with benefits", they aren't dating, they are only physically attracted to each other for the purpose of sex alone. These category of youths can even be dating other people but come together on mutual agreement to have sex.

Youths disregard biblical warnings considering premarital sex as a sin before God, they can repent temporarily in church as a result of the spiritual euphoria but afterwards they give in to fleshly lusts, the pleasure is just so overwhelming.

Beyond the pleasure there are several benefits for having sex, medical reports indicate that having sex at least once a week is an effective remedy for relieving stress.

Endorphins and oxytocin are released during sex, and these feel-good hormones activate pleasure centers in the brain that create feelings of intimacy and relaxation and help stave off anxiety and depression, says WH advisor Laura Berman, Ph.D., an assistant clinical professor of ob-gyn and psychiatry at the Feinberg School of Medicine at Northwestern University and author of *It's Not Him, It's You!*

According to web md, sex also boosts one's immune system, lowers blood pressure, Lowers risks of heart attack, boosts self-esteem and reduces prostate cancer risk. I wouldn't want to dispute that since I am a medical student but beyond the benefits, there are negative consequences as well such as increased risks of sexually transmitted diseases especially among adventurous youths who love to explore and have sex with any one they possibly can.

Gird Your Mind

There are also chances of unwanted pregnancies which can lead to death in cases when the lady out of desperation resorts to abortion in the hands of unqualified personnels.

But what is God's purpose for sex?

Having an understanding of God's purpose for sex beyond the usual indulging in premarital sex is a sin youths hear in church could perhaps help to turn their minds in the right direction.

The paragraphs highlighted below taken from an online article, God's purpose for sex and marriage explains this.

Sex was created by God to be practiced within the confines of marriage for the purpose of procreation alone. God designed human reproduction through sex as a means to populate the earth. But His eventual intent is to bring as many of the billions who have been born – those who will repent – into His family as spiritual children. In a sense He, too, is reproducing Himself.

Therefore, we can see that reproduction of human beings has two purposes – to give physical life now to our posterity and to provide the potential for many children of God to receive eternal spirit life.

God created a continuing sexual interest and sexual appeal in human beings. This in itself is a healthy trait of the human mind and is triggered by hormones that God designed the body to produce.

God created this sustained interest in sex as a means for men and women to express love in marriage.
This is one of the great purposes for sex that many have failed to understand.

That sex is a means of expressing love is made plain in Paul's epistle to the Ephesians. "Husbands, love your wives, just as Christ also loved the church, and gave Himself for her, … that she should be holy and without blemish. So husbands ought to love their wives as their own bodies … For this reason a man shall leave his father and mother and be joined to his wife, and the two shall become one flesh" (Ephesians 5: 25–31 NKJV).
What does Paul say is the purpose of marriage and of becoming one flesh through sex? The purpose is love.

To broaden your knowledge on this, check the reference included at the back page of this book "God's purpose for sex and marriage."

Youths are rarely driven or motivated by love. Sex among youths, in present times, is more like an exchange market between guys and girls. Both parties obtain maximum satisfaction. The guy feels like a champion who has just conquered a city and goes about boasting to his friends, who, most times, feel happier than the guy who engaged in the act. To him and his friends, the girl is cheap; the girl, in turn, feels happy that at least he bought her the new phone or bag she wanted before having his way with her. To her, he is just someone who can cater to her numerous needs. There is no actual love between them; what they feel is temporary infatuation that dies off after their libidinal urges are satisfied.

However, some girls develop genuine feelings for the boy, whose sole aim is just to have his way with her. She ends up being heartbroken and then goes about saying all guys are the same. To avoid the heartbreak, it's best to focus on building yourself and being the best you can be. Don't be easily deceived; true love is rare to find among youths.

"Many a man claims to have unfailing love, but a faithful man who can find?" (Proverbs 20: 6 NIV)

The Bible talked about David's son, Tamar, who initially loved his sister and then hated her after he forcefully slept with her. It also happens in our world today; a guy can profess all the love in the world to you and then hate you after he sleeps with you.

Some women justify their claims for getting into a relationship and giving themselves out cheaply because most guys will want to sleep with them before they get married to them. That is totally wrong and unreasonable. After the gratification of the sexual desire, there is nothing else to explore or wait for. The next thing is a gradual degeneration of the relationship. The key to a lasting relationship is to wait, think, pray, and watch. As you do this, certain realities become exposed and you get to understand your partner more. Trust me, he will value you more if you deprive him of the sex till you are officially married.

Also, don't allow your desire to get married – because your mates are getting married – drive you into making the wrong decision. Settle for a guy who can care for you, nurture you, and transform and bring out the best in you just like Christ does for his bride, the Church.

But, at the same time, the truth must be told. Women cause the majority of their problems. They put on skimpy wears in the name of dressing to look hot, forgetting that guys are easily moved by what they see. You can't keep a yam in front of a goat and expect the goat not to eat it.

Song of Solomon 8: 4 (KJV) says, "Daughters of Jerusalem, I charge you: do not arouse or awaken love until it so desires."

What a lady puts on can cloud a guy's sense of judgment. Infatuation builds up, he mistakes it for love, and then he transmits those feelings to the lady in question, who receives them. Her limbic system acts on them and opens up her emotions to the guy, who plays with them, and in the end, she is heartbroken.

For a while, I paused here and told the Lord that I wouldn't write this book, because quite a number of girls have had their hearts broken on my account. Ladies fell into my hands easily like fruits off trees, and I took advantage of them; that was one of the devil's schemes to keep me away from God.

The good thing about Christianity or being called into ministry is that, when the Lord visits you, he changes everything about you completely. I know it's difficult to stay away from premarital sex, but you can if you allow God, alone, to nurture you. The anointing of God is greater than any addiction.

A pastor I knew, while I was in Republic of Benin, used to say, and I quote, "When you encounter Christ, your sexual desires will be made Godly." This very man of God, Pastor Layo, gave up practicing law upon graduation to become a pastor, and he is still transforming the lives of many in Cotonou, Republic of Benin.

Joel Osteen said that the way we get empowered for the day is through our union with God. Union can be likened to a marriage, and a good marriage is successful when both parties spend time with each other.

"But thanks be to God, that though you used to be slaves to sin, you wholeheartedly obeyed the form of teaching to which you were entrusted. You have been set free from sin and have become slaves to righteousness" (Romans 6: 17–18 NIV).

"Therefore brethren, we are debtors, not to the flesh, to live after the flesh. For if ye live after the flesh, ye shall die: but if ye through the spirit do mortify the deeds of the body, ye shall live" (Romans 8: 12–13 KJV).

"We are no longer under the law but under grace, this is the dispensation of being led by the spirit.

"This I say then, walk in the spirit, and ye shall not fulfil the lust of the flesh" (Galatians 5: 16 KJV).

"You however are controlled not by the sinful nature but by the spirit, if the spirit of God lives in you. And if anyone does not have the spirit of Christ, he does not belong to Christ. But if Christ is in you, your body is dead because of sin, yet your spirit is alive because of righteousness. And if the spirit of him who raised Jesus from the dead is living in you, he who raised Christ from the dead will also give life to your mortal bodies through his spirit, who lives in you" (Romans 8: 9–11 NIV).

Spend quality time in prayer and in studying the Word of God, and he will give you the grace to flee from sexual immorality.

The new creation has the ability to live above sin through the help of the Holy Spirit that is at work in him. Therefore, he does not live a lifestyle of sin. Although he might fall into sin occasionally, he doesn't go on sinning, because God's seed remains in him, and even if he does fall into sin, he has the grace to ask for forgiveness and get it right again with the father, because he now lives a life created after God in righteousness and holiness."

—Pastor Sola Idowu

Chasing after Wealth

This is one thing many youths channel all their energy into, and this is another strategy the devil employs in keeping youths away from serving God. I wasn't an exception. At one point in my life, the only thing I cared about was money. I couldn't say anything without talking about money. My family and friends can testify to this. I am only proud of myself for one reason: as much as I loved money, I also loved to help people. I derive joy in solving people's problems, and that's how the dream to become a senator came alive within me.

There is nothing wrong in desiring to be successful or to have money. It only becomes wrong when the love for money leads you into doing terrible and unthinkable things, as is the case with most youths today.

Let me quote what the Lord said to Kenneth Hagin: "I am not opposed to my children being rich; I am only opposed to them being coveters."

"For the love of money is a root of all kinds of evil. Some people, eager for money have wandered from the faith and pierced themselves with many griefs" (1 timothy 6: 10 NIV).

"Whoever loves money never has money enough; whoever loves wealth is never satisfied with his income. This too is meaningless" Ecclesiastes 5: 10 NIV).

As youths, everything we see easily moves us. We want to buy every fanciful thing we lay our eyes on. It's not wrong to buy new things if we can afford them and still be in a state of financial homeostasis, but it's unreasonable if we allow our quest for material things to lead us to stealing or borrowing money and running into debts.

Don't compete with your peers to use the most expensive phone, drive a car, buy the most expensive shoes, or fix the most expensive hair (as in the case of ladies). Do these things only if, within yourself, you know you can afford to do them. There is no express train to success. My mum has always told me that the world could be likened to a table fan. It can blow in your direction for some time and then blow in your neighbour's direction the next minute. One only has to be patient, work hard, and trust God, and the good things of life will come knocking at your door.

The Bible says "For promotion cometh neither from the east, nor from the west, nor from the south. But God is the judge: he putteth down one and setteth up another" psalms 75:6-7 KJV.

God wants to lead us in the path of promotion. He has a purpose and destiny for our lives, and he wants us to enter into it. Often, we may go through the path of trials and tribulations in order to be shaped and refined to enter into the destiny God has prepared for us. God leads us through a path of distress and discipline, which can be painful, but it will always be worth it. The process takes us to our promotion.

The problem with us today is that we want the promotion without the process; God does not do things that way, for he isn't a man.

"For my thoughts are not your thoughts, neither are your ways my ways, saith the Lord" (Isaiah 55: 8 KJV).

A man may promote you today and demote you tomorrow for no just reason, but God promotes or demotes in line with his purpose for our lives.

"For I know the thoughts that I think towards you, saith the lord, thoughts of peace, and not of evil, to give you an expected end" (Jeremiah 29: 11 KJV).

It is now left to us to trust and obey him and he will uplift us. If you are faithful over a few things, he will make you ruler over many things as illustrated in (Matthew 25: 21).

"Keep your lives free from the love of money and be content with what you have, because God has said, never will I leave you; never will I forsake you" (Hebrews 13: 5 NIV).

"Therefore do not be anxious, saying, what shall we eat? Or what shall we drink? or what shall we wear? For the gentiles seek after all these things, and your heavenly father knows that you need them all. But seek first the kingdom of God and his righteousness, and all these things will be added to you" (Matthew 6: 31–33 ESV).

These are the Words of the Lord, and the Bible made us to understand that his Word does not return to him void. Learn to be content, and let God be the source of your income.

God's Expectation for Youths

While we were still in primary school and at some point in high school, we put in our best towards our academics. We knew our parents expected much from us, so we didn't want to disappoint them.

God, our Heavenly Father, also does not want us to disappoint him. Having outlined the factors that drive youths far from worshipping God, I believe if you can avoid these things, you will be in close proximity with God and therefore placed in a position where he can help you discover your purpose (his plans for you) or instruct someone to help you identify it. The former is better; hearing directly from God is an advantage you can have over the non-believer.

There is a sense of fulfilment when you discover your purpose. One day in surgery class, when we were learning to stitch, I jokingly asked my friend which is easier: to say be healed in the name of Jesus or to cut the person up, remove the tumour, and start stitching up the patient again? My friend laughed at me and said none of us can exercise that kind of authority, that it would take a long time, and that I was just being unrealistic. I refused to accept what he said. I told him my purpose was to save lives and that it didn't matter if I adopted the spiritual means by speaking words of faith or the physical means by playing the role of a surgeon.

Moreover, the Bible makes us understand that we were created in God's image, which means the life of God, the very DNA of God was infused into our spirit man, implying that we are gods, and we are meant to function like gods on earth.

God wants us to stop focusing on our faults, failures, and mistakes and look unto his love that never fails.

"And their sins and iniquities will I remember no more" (Hebrews 10: 17 KJV).

Put the Lord first if you want to succeed in whatever you set out to do. The Bible says in acts 17:28 NIV, "For in him we live and move and have our being." He gives us a sense of direction if we have a longing for him.

God wants us to take our academics seriously and develop our minds; we need to be academically sound to function spiritually.

Education is the greatest asset any nation can boast of; God wants youths to develop the zeal to acquire knowledge, read biographies of great men who have succeeded in the fields we are interested in, and learn from the antecedents and intricacies of their lives. I read *Think Big* by Ben Carson. Today he is celebrated as one of the best neurosurgeons on earth for being the first to successfully separate Siamese twins, but it wouldn't have been so if his mum hadn't talked sense into him and if he hadn't held on to God. A guy who was considered a dummy by everyone for having the lowest marks in any class test or exam suddenly developed interest in studying and went on to outshine his peers. Ben Carson said his mum told him and his elder brother Curtis that the Lord had spoken to her and told her things to do to improve some situations in their family. One of the decisions she made was that both boys would have to read two books every week, learn all the new words, and submit a summary of the books in writing to her. Initially they did it just to impress their mum, but afterwards, they started enjoying it and looked forward to studying. And that was what transformed Ben Carson. He went from being a poor student to receiving honours.

It made me remember my own dad; he instilled the reading culture in me. I may not be the best, but when they want to mention students who are great readers and who do well in school, my name will be mentioned. It's nothing compared to the dreams and aspirations I have for myself and God's plans for my life. I owe my parents a lot, especially my dad for setting me on the right track. As a clinical psychologist who studied in the United States, he was able to understand me, and he was constantly pushing me to succeed. He taught me that there is no limitation to what my mind can achieve, and once I set my mind to do something, I can achieve it through God's help. He didn't let my siblings and me watch much TV when he was around. He would always ask us why we wasted our creative time watching other people when we should be trying to develop our own minds and thinking of ways to make an impact in our world. My brother and I saved up money and got ourselves a Sega console. My dad walked in one Saturday morning, disconnected the game, and smashed it to pieces right in front of our eyes. On another occasion, he came in and saw us watching a movie. I guess he didn't like the idea of exposing our minds to people killing for fun at our young age. He walked right up to the CD player, brought out the CD, and broke it to pieces.

It hurt us very much. We thought he was being very hard on us, but now, considering the way he brought us up and the fact that children of most politicians don't do very well academically, I am glad he pushed us that much.

Take your studies seriously and develop your minds so that you can function better in the area of influence the Lord has called you to. Benjamin Franklin said, "A learned blockhead is a greater blockhead than an ignorant one." Always remember that the world is in need of learned men and women who can make a difference, not just graduates who wasted their time in school.

Think of King Solomon when he became king of Israel. The first thing he asked God for was wisdom to govern Israel. The Lord God was impressed and not only gave him wisdom but also prosperity.

The Master Jesus, as a boy, knew the importance of knowledge; he sat among the priests in the temple to learn of them. This knowledge never departed from him. He referred to the knowledge he had acquired each time the Pharisees came up with their unnecessary arguments.

Apostle Paul, too, was chosen to preach God's Word, because he was educated and could put up arguments when the need arose.

"Get wisdom, get understanding; do not forget my words or swerve from them. Do not forsake wisdom and she will protect you; love her and she will watch over you. Wisdom is supreme; therefore get wisdom. Though it cost all you have, get understanding. Esteem her and she will exalt you; embrace her and she will honour you. She will set a garland of grace on your head and present you with a crown of splendor" (Proverbs 4: 5–9 NIV).

Now you see why God wants you to take our studies seriously in other to function better in the accomplishment of your purpose.

Have a vision of your goals. Lawrence J. Peter said, "If you don't know where you are going, you will end up someplace else."

Habakkuk 2: 2–3 KJV states, "Write the vision, and make it plain upon tables, that he may run that readeth it. For the vision is for an appointed time, but at the end it shall speak, and not lie: though it tarry, wait for it; because it will surely come, it will not tarry."

God wants you to visualize a life of your wildest dreams. When you were a child, what was it you said you would be? Now is the time to reawaken that vision and break it down into actions that you can take one step at a time.

If you want a thing bad enough to go out and fight for it, to work day and night for it, to give up your time, your peace and sleep for it. If all that you dream and scheme is about it, and life seems useless and worthless without it, if you gladly sweat for it, and fret for it and plan for it and lose all your terror of the opposition for it.

If you simply go for that thing that you want with all your capacity, strength and sagacity, faith, hope and confidence and stern pertinacity. If neither cold, poverty, famine, nor gout, sickness nor pain of body and brain, can keep you away from the thing that you want, if dogged and grim you beseech and beset it, with the help of God, you will get it! — The will to win by Berton Braley

God wants us to accept ourselves for who we are; we all are unique in our different ways. Who says we must be tall, short, fair, dark, or of a particular gender in order to attain greatness? The first step towards attaining greatness is to break that barrier of inequality in our minds. Learn to accept yourself.

Silence the negative voice of criticism and disbelief in your mind that you can't do a thing. If you acquire all the knowledge and skills in the world but don't believe in yourself, you will certainly fail.

Our Lord Jesus said, "And if a house be divided against itself, that house cannot stand." Mark 3:25 KJV

"Continuous effort – not strength or intelligence is the key to unlocking our potential." —Winston Churchill

God wants you to be in good health, according to 3 John 1: 2 (KJV). "Beloved I wish above all things that thou mayest prosper and be in health even as thy soul prospereth."

Maintain a proper hygiene, and engage in bodily exercise every day to be in a state of good health. You cannot fulfil God's purpose if you have a deteriorating health condition that you can avoid on your own.

Physical exercise is any bodily activity that enhances or maintains overall health and wellness. Perform it to strengthen muscles and the cardiovascular system or for weight loss or maintenance.

I don't let a day pass without consuming green tea and doing push-ups or indoor exercises. Green tea contains polyphenols – natural antioxidants that prevent cancer, improve blood flow, and reduce cholesterol levels.

Frequent and regular exercise boosts the immune system and helps prevent cardiovascular diseases, type 2 diabetes, and obesity. It also improves mental health, helps prevent depression, and helps to promote or maintain positive self-esteem.

Researches have also proven that exercise reduces the risk of dementia and enhances cognitive function.

Why is God insisting that we be in good health? Man is a spirit being with a soul residing in a mortal body.
Vine's dictionary of Greek words as cited in an online bible study defines "the soul as the seat of intellect: the seat of the sentient element by which he perceives, reflects, feels, and desires". The soul is the place that houses our will, our emotions, and our intellect (the thinking, reasoning part of us: the mind).

Now you see why God wants us to be in good health. Without your physical body being in a state of functional homeostasis, in the sense that you are in good health and free from any infirmity hindering you from communicating to God, it will be difficult for your soul and spirit to function effectively.

Now you understand that your soul is your mind. Your soul can prosper through what you let in or absorb.

"Do not conform any longer to the pattern of this world, but be ye transformed by the renewing of your mind. Then you will be able to test and approve what God's will is – his good, pleasing and perfect will" (Romans 12: 2 NIV).

"The upright (honorable, intrinsically good) man out of the good treasure (stored) in his heart produces what is upright (honorable and intrinsically good), and the evil man out of the evil storehouse brings forth that which is depraved (wicked and intrinsically evil); for out of the abundance (overflow) of the heart his mouth speaks" (Luke 6: 45 AB).

In a nutshell, what we believe in our hearts and what we think in our minds are what we will speak out and talk about. Therefore, if we want to experience the blessings of God in our lives, it is vital that we speak forth health, provision, prosperity, freedom from affliction, and depression.

To ensure that our souls prosper, we should study and meditate on the Word of God.

"When you study the word of God, it makes you what it talks about." —Pastor Chris Oyakilome

"Wherefore lay apart all filthiness and superfluity of naughtiness, and receive with meekness the engrafted word, which is able to save your souls" (James 1: 21 KJV).

When you do this (prosper your soul through the Word of God) and keep your body in good health, you will see massive changes in every area of your life.

God wants you to learn to manage your time wisely. Effective leaders, in the world today, are men and women who have learned to manage their time wisely. It is a primary secret to anyone's success. Time management is the act or process of planning and exercising conscious control over the amount of time spent on specific activities, especially to increase effectiveness, efficiency, or productivity. You can manage your time like I have learnt to by setting priorities and goals according to degree of importance and eliminating tasks that don't add value to your life. Remember, world leaders, too, have the same twenty-four hours in a day that you and I have. The difference between them and us is that they have learnt to manage theirs. So quit complaining that you are choked up with time, and learn how to manage your time towards accomplishing your purpose.

Do what you need to do, without making excuses and without procrastination.

"Time makes heroes but dissolves celebrities." —Daniel J. Boorstin

"He, who every morning plans the transaction of the day and follows out that plan, carries a thread that will guide him through a labyrinth of the most busy life." —Victor Hugo

We realize our dilemma goes deeper than the shortage of time; it is basically a problem of priorities. We confess we have left undone those things we ought to have done and we have done those things which we ought not to have done." —Charles E. Hummel

"Time is the coin of your life. It is the only coin you can have and only you can determine how it will be spent. Be careful lest you let other people spend it for you." —Carl Sandburg

Mastering your time is something you can work on if you are to accomplish your purpose. Remind yourself each day that you may not have time but you ought to create time. You must govern the clock and not be governed by it.

The last thing God desires from us is that we learn to follow the inward witness, the Holy Spirit whom he has given to every believer. How can you tell if the spirit is leading you? It is evident in the fruits of your life – your attitude and actions.

Galatians 5: 22–23 (KJV) says, "But the fruit of the spirit is love, joy, peace, long suffering, gentleness, goodness and faith, meekness, temperance: against such there is no law."

Our lives would be much better if we learn to follow the leading of the Holy Spirit. "Youths", have an advantage of being young and learning to follow the leading of the Holy Spirit is the secret to long-term success.

"I have taught you wisdom and the right way to live. Nothing will stand in your way if you walk wisely, and you will not stumble when you run" (Proverbs 4: 11–12 GNB).

"Wisdom is making decisions today based on knowing what will happen tomorrow. Wisdom brings the flow of God's blessings in your life and it will cause you to see the power of God in your life through the gifts of the spirit."
—Tom Brown

One of the best things to have is the wisdom of God to make the right decisions, and this comes through being led by the spirit. You don't have to be in the dark anymore concerning your future. The Holy Spirit will guide you based on what is yet to come.

Reward for Holding on to Christ

While growing up I received several revelations from different ministers all stating that I had been called into ministry, but I was too stubborn to acknowledge what they were telling me. I had an erroneous impression that pastors were poor people because of the ones I had seen in the marketplace, carrying Bibles around. Little did I know that they were simply spreading the gospel. I picked offence whenever they called me a pastor or an evangelist. I was like, "How can you people tell me I will be a preacher? I want to be a politician and acquire wealth so I can serve humanity."

I left Nigeria for Ukraine, with the intention to study medicine and live my normal life as just an occasional church attendee on Sundays. Little did I know that the Lord had different plans for me. People came to my hostel room regularly to preach the gospel, and as a result, I returned their visits by worshipping in their various churches in a bid to find where I would finally settle.

My story changed, one day, when I attended a worker's retreat, organized by the fellowship where I belong. I wasn't in the church work force; I was only invited by my friend. I intentionally came late for the program, but it didn't stop God from arresting me. The Lord announced me that day in the presence of his people. A woman, who is now a doctor, was leading a prayer session, when suddenly she said something that shocked everyone. She said, "God is telling me that there is someone in our midst who will be as great as Evangelist Reinhard Bonnke and take the gospel to every corner of the earth." Then she turned and pointed at me. It wasn't a surprise, because, like I mentioned before, ministers had been giving me revelations. But it shocked me because I never believed God's presence could dwell mightily among students. Also, I didn't expect God to compare me with Reinhard Bonnke; that guy has done so much in propagating the gospel. Where was I supposed to start from to get to the height he had reached? That was what ran through my mind, but it dawned on me that the Lord was serious and that he, indeed, wanted to work with me. Afterwards, another friend of mine made sure I joined the evangelism team. And the friend who invited me to the workers retreat, who has also played a major role, so far, in my spiritual growth, made sure I joined the Bible study team. And that was how the transformation started.

There have been challenges, when temptations have come from different corners to overshadow me. I've given in to some of them; still, each time I fall short, the Lord gives me double strength to stand on my feet. He can also do the same for you if you will let him take his place in your life.

Beloved there are several benefits for anyone who makes the right decision to welcome Christ into his life.

1) You receive the person of the Holy Ghost, who becomes your guide, your comforter, and your teacher.

Permit me to paraphrase what Kenneth Hagin said in his sermon on how to be led by the spirit "If you have the Holy Ghost in you, you wouldn't need to consult human counselors, for the Holy Ghost will teach you all things. All you need to do is to get acquainted with him."

"But the counselor, the Holy Spirit whom the father will send in my name, will teach you all things and will remind of everything I have said to you" (John 14: 26 NIV).

2) You receive an overdose of grace to do things excellently and exceptionally.

"And we know that in all things God works for the good of those who love him, who have been called according to his purpose" (Romans 8: 28 NIV).

"But to each one of us grace has been given as Christ apportioned it" (Ephesians 4: 7 NIV).

3) You become recognized by God as pointed out in 1 Corinthians 8: 2–3. NKJV "And if anyone thinks that he knows anything, he knows nothing yet as he ought to know. But if anyone loves God, this one is known by Him.

4) You automatically become an adopted child of God, a new gene. The seed of God comes into you.

"Since, then, you have been raised with Christ, set your hearts on things above, where Christ is seated at the right hand of God. Set your minds on things above, not on earthly things. For you died and your life is now hidden with Christ in God" (Colossians 3: 1–3 NIV).

5) You automatically start bearing fruits by abiding in Christ.

"Remain in me and I will remain in you. No branch can bear fruit by itself; it must remain in the vine. Neither can you bear fruit unless you remain in me" (John 15: 4 NIV).

"The righteous will flourish like a palm tree, they will grow like a cedar of Lebanon; planted in the house of the Lord, they will flourish in the courts of our God. They will still bear fruits in old age; they will still stay fresh and green" (Psalm 92: 12–14 NIV).

On this note, everything you touch prospers, including your academics and finances.

I usually boast aloud to people that I can't be broke, not because my parents are very wealthy or because I have a regular inflow of money but because I am connected to the source of all wealth. His name is Jehovah Jireh, the great provider.

Many times my friends see me and tell me that I'm looking good or that they like what I'm putting on, and then I reply in Igbo (owu aka oru Jehovah), meaning it is the Lord's doing.

My little secret is in paying tithes and seed sowing. When you sow into the Lord's vineyard, you will reap bountifully.

Seed sowing is a principle that has never failed. When I was a little boy, the only scripture I held on to was what I had read about God being pleased with Abel's offering. It has been the sole reason why I sow into God's vineyard at every opportunity, and God has blessed me immeasurably on each occasion.

As naïve I was then, I had received a twenty-naira note that I was supposed to share with my immediate elder brother, and I had convinced him that we should burn it as an offering to the Lord. I told him we kept hearing, in Sunday school, about men who offered burnt offerings to the Lord and said that we should sacrifice to the Lord too. He bought the idea, so we lit a match and burnt that money. It wasn't the right thing to do, because money was meant to buy things or put directly into the church's offering box. But, since we were limited by our understanding as children, the Lord acted on our ignorance, and that very day, someone else gave us twenty naira each.

That's just a simple illustration but in the reality of it, God looks at the simplicity of the heart and the motive behind any action. You must not give God money only; he is not really interested in your money, for he is the one who provided the money. All he wants is for you to see him as the source of your income and return a tenth back to him for his work on earth. You can also invest your time; the Lord looks at every form of selfless service you render, and he rewards you for it. (He causes you to bear fruits.)

6) You are fully equipped to resist and defeat the devil as seen in Ephesians 6: 10–17.

7) You are empowered to do greater works as seen in John 14: 12.

8) You come under the protective covering of God as seen in Isaiah 54: 17 and Psalm 105: 15.

9) You are lifted up when others are cast down as seen in Job 22: 29.

You succeed in places people fail – things considered difficult by the normal human mind become a walkover for you.

The importance of studying the Word and becoming rooted in Christ cannot be overemphasized.

In biochemistry, we were made to understand that the body stores up glucose as glycogen, so, in cases of starvation or glucose deprivation, the body utilizes its glycogen reserves stored in muscle and liver cells. When it is finished, it makes use of ketone bodies. That's the same thing the Word of God does in cases of depression, anxiety, stress, and various life struggles: the Word of God you have stored in your spirit man comes alive and gives you the spiritual energy you require to pass through any challenge. God's Word never fails.

I've witnessed something through my days of working out at the gym. The instructor stands behind me when I am lifting weights. He is there to assist me when the weight gets too heavy and I need to drop and readjust myself. God did the same thing for us. He sent his Son to die for us (Romans 5: 8), and his death paved the way for God to send the Holy Spirit. When we accept him, he gives us himself in the person of the Holy Ghost, our gym instructor, who helps us in our difficulties. He helps us do things that we cannot do with our own might.

In the same way, the Spirit helps us in our weaknesses. "We do not know what we ought to pray for, but the spirit himself intercedes for us with groans that words cannot express" (Romans 8: 26 NIV).

What are you waiting for? The Bible pointed out, in Romans 8: 19, that "The earnest expectation of the creature waiteth for the manifestation of the sons of God."

We hear these things on a daily basis. How long will it take us to act on them?

The world has been waiting for you to harness the potentials the Lord has imbedded in you for the good of all humanity. What better way to do that than to lean unto God himself, the source of the vision, the author, and the finisher of our faith.

"Therefore brothers and sisters, since we have confidence to enter the most holy place by the blood of Jesus, by a new and living way opened for us through the curtain, that is his body, and since we have a great priest over the house of God, let us draw near to God with a sincere heart in full assurance of faith, having our hearts sprinkled to cleanse us from a guilty conscience and having our bodies washed with pure water. Let us hold unswervingly to the hope we profess, for he who promised is faithful. And let us consider how we may spur one another on towards love and good deeds. Let us not give up meeting together, as some are in the habit of doing, but let us encourage one another and all the more as you see the day approaching. If we deliberately keep on sinning after we have received the knowledge of the truth, no sacrifice for sins is left, but only a fearful expectation of judgment and of raging fire that will consume the enemies of God" (Hebrews 10: 19–27 NIV).

It is God's desire that you accept Christ, and through constant prayer, you will come to an understanding of his Word and watch it produce results in your life.

Turning impossibility to possibility

How many of your goals? How many of your aspirations or objectives have been buried only because of this word impossibility?

Are you still in the bondage of sin because someone said to you at a time that it is not possible to live a holy life?

This word has made the grave yard richer than the oil fields or even gold mines, because many great ideas, man visions and goals that would have been actualized died with the man and was buried with the man.

In 1870 the Methodists in Indiana in US held a national conference in a college, the president of the college said to the presiding bishop, I think we live in a very exciting age.

"What do you see?" the bishop asked.

He replied, "I believe we are coming to a time of great inventions. I believe also that men will fly through the air like birds."

The bishop said to him, "The air is reserved for angels and birds. There should be no room for such crazy ideas in this place.

But the president replied, "Sir, I believe it is possible."

The name of the president was Milton Wright and his two sons with him were Wilber and Orville Wright. His sons took the vision and pursued it, till they invented the aero plane. Today man flies even better than the birds.

In 1870 that was an impossibility, but events of today are showing us that so-called impossibilities are possible.

What men have told you is impossible, God has a word for it, and you can find it in Luke 1: 37: "For nothing will be impossible with God."

Nebuchadnezzar's Dream

"In the second year of his reign, Nebuchadnezzar had dreams; his mind was troubled and he could not sleep. So the king summoned the magicians, enchanters, sorcerers and astrologers to tell him what he had dreamed. When they came in and stood before the king, he said to them, 'I have had a dream and it troubles me and I want to know what it means.'

"Then the astrologers answered the king in Aramaic, 'O king, live forever! Tell your servants the dream, and we will interpret it.'

"The king replied to the astrologers, 'This is what I have firmly decided: If you do not tell me what my dream was and interpret it, I will have you cut into pieces and your houses turned into piles of rubble. But if you tell me the dream and explain it, you will receive from me gifts and rewards and great honour. So tell me the dream and interpret it for me.'

"Once more they replied, 'Let the king tell his servants the dream and we will interpret it.'

"Then the king answered, 'I am certain that you are trying to gain time, because you realize that this is what I have firmly decided:

"'If you do not tell me the dream, there is just one penalty for you. You have conspired to tell me misleading and wicked things, hoping the situation will change. So then, tell me the dream, and I will know that you can interpret it for me.'

"The astrologers answered the king; 'there is not a man on earth who can do what the king asks! No king, however great and mighty has ever asked such a thing of any magician or enchanter or astrologer.

"'What the king asks is too difficult. No one can reveal it to the king except the gods, and they do not live among men'" (Daniel 2: 1–11 NIV).

Highlight verses ten and eleven, and read all the way down.

"Then king Nebuchadnezzar fell prostrate before Daniel and paid him honor and ordered that an offering and incense be presented to him.

"The king said to Daniel, 'Surely your God is the God of gods and the Lord of kings and a revealer of mysteries, for you were able to reveal this mystery'" (Daniel 2: 46–47 NIV).

Daniel was not an astrologer, a magician, or a sorcerer, but he turned what others called impossibility into possibility through God's help.

Gideon's Victory from Judges 7: 1–15

The Lord reduced their military strength from thirty-two thousand soldiers to ten thousand and then to three hundred. God wanted to prove to Gideon that he is a God of possibilities. God wants the glory to be ascribed to him alone at all times as we read in verse 2.

People have given up on cases, but with God, there will always be a possibility as seen in John 11: 1–45: Jesus learnt that Lazarus was sick but chose not to go until after four days, when he had been dead and buried. The lesson that God is teaching us is that there is no case that is dead and buried in our lives.

For you, as a believer, to move from the realm of impossibility to possibility, there are things you must do.

1) You must come to an understanding of who God is, in other words, have a relationship with the God that makes all things possible. Obey his laws. God actually emphasized this when he said to Joshua in the book of Joshua chapter one and verse eight: "This book of the law shall not depart out of thy mouth but thou shall meditate therein day and night, that thou mayest observe to do according to all

that is written therein: for then thou shall make thy way prosperous and thou shall have good success."

Just like fish cannot survive without water and plants can't survive without good soil, humans cannot survive without God. The Bible says without God, you can do nothing. Success cannot be bought; it can only be acquired. In other words, success depends on you getting close to the Lord and obeying his laws as stated in his Word.

2) learn to isolate yourself from wordliness. It is not enough to know and believe in God; you must also make a firm decision to set yourself apart for him. It has to do with renewal of the mind. You must be free from sin and worldliness.

"And be not conformed to this world: but be ye transformed by the renewing of your mind, that ye may prove what is that good, and acceptable, and perfect, will of God" (Romans 12: 2 KJV).

3) Refuse to be discouraged by the failure of others. The fact that others have failed does not mean that you will fail. The fact that those you consider better off than you does not imply that you will not make it, because you are a unique

person. The Spirit of God that lives in you is the Spirit of possibilities. He is the God before whom nothing shall be impossible.

4) Be patient with the God of possibilities as you lean on him with confidence. Daniel did not only know this God of possibilities, Daniel did not only set himself apart for him, Daniel was also patient with God. Daniel 2: 16–22 NIV

Also consider the prophet Elijah when he was praying for the rain to come. He was patient with God. He knew whom he was calling upon. Seven times he sent out his servant to check for the rain, and each time his servant reported there was no rain, he would go down on his knees again and pray. 1 Kings 18:42–45

Mark 11: 23 NIV says, "Truly I tell you, if anyone says to this mountain, 'Go, throw yourself into the sea', and does not doubt in his heart but believes that what he says will happen, it will be done for them."

The mountain does not have to move immediately. Your duty is to speak to the mountain. It is not your business to know when and how it will be removed. God can use your friends, your parents, or your enemies. Don't look at how it will be removed; just speak to the spiritual mountain of impossibility.

5) Be prayerful for your impossibility to turn to possibilities. Nothing is impossible; just pray and trust God. If one had predicted that a black man would lead the United States, it would have been countered, but today it is so. God turns things around when you pray.

For the original article without the author's words, check the reference at the back of the book.

How many of you know of Martin Luther King? He is celebrated as a freedom fighter by the Neo Black Movement of Africa. He was an American pastor. He was assassinated for his dreams.

"I have a dream that one day this nation will rise up and live out the true meaning of its creed. We hold these truths to be self-evident that all men are created equal. Martin luther king

"I have a dream that one day, down in Alabama, with its vicious racists, with its governor having his lips dripping with the words of 'interposition' and nullification – one day right there in Alabama little black boys and girls will be able to join hands with little white boys and white girls as brothers and sisters." Martin luther king

Today America is an anti-racial nation. Be focused when you have a dream; pray about it, and then pursue it.

See today as the beginning of a new you, the start of new opportunities to what you should be. What you are now is not your best. You have a potential, a seed for greater achievement locked within your consciousness. Bring it out and be what you are designed to be, achieve what you can achieve. The Holy Bible says, 'As a man thinketh in his heart, so is he.' It does not say, 'so will he be' but 'so is he.' It is already manifested in the spiritual realm. It is already present.

"Ye are the salt of the earth: but if the salt has lost his savour, wherewith shall it be salted? It is thenceforth good for nothing, but to be cast out, and be trodden under foot of men. Ye are the light of the world. A city set on an hill cannot be hid" (Matthew 5: 13–14 KJV).

As God's children, our lights are meant to shine so that the world can see and give glory to our Heavenly Father.

It reminds me of a quote by Marianne Williamson also used by Nelson Mandela: "Our deepest fear is not that we are inadequate. Our deepest fear is that we are powerful beyond measure. It is our light, not our darkness that frightens us most. We ask ourselves, who am I to be brilliant, gorgeous, talented and famous? Actually who are you not to be? You are a child of God. Your playing small does not serve the world. There is nothing enlightened about shrinking so that people won't feel insecure around you. We were born to make manifest the glory of God that is within us. It's not just in some of us; it's in all of us. And when we let our own light shine, we unconsciously give other people permission to do the same. As we are liberated from our own fear, our presence automatically liberates others."

I heard this quote for the first time in the movie *Akeelah and the Bee* about a young girl who was good at spelling words. She wasn't discouraged by the fact that she schooled in a poor school, that her dad was late, or that her mum was unsupportive at first. She was determined to win the contest, and she did, though she had help along the line from a coach and friends.

The storyline is that you can overcome life's obstacles and challenges if you are determined and have self-confidence. When I finished the movie, I went out, printed that quote, and pasted it on the wall of my room in Nigeria so I could read it every morning when I woke up.

Another movie I learnt a lot from is the Japanese cartoon *Naruto*. It tells the story of an orphan boy neglected by the entire village because of the circumstances that surrounded his birth. He was branded an outcast. As a result, he resorted to mischief in order to attract notice; still, people considered him a nuisance. In the ninja academy, he was the last in class. He was mocked and laughed at, but one thing kept him going: his innermost passion, zeal, and goal to become the Hokage – the strongest ninja in the village. That sole dream caused him to train harder, and eventually, the entire ninja world acknowledged and respected him.

Don't ever dwell on that word impossibility for any reason. The world of sports previously believed that no one could completely run a mile in less than four minutes. Roger Bannister stepped forward and proved everyone wrong by completing that distance in three minutes, fifty-nine seconds. The significant thing about it is that, since then, twenty thousand people have done it, including high school students. What changed? When they got on the track, they knew it had been done, so they didn't see it as impossible anymore. So they did it. Visualize that dream of yours, and make it a reality, even if you will be the first person to do it.

"If God wants you to do something, He will give you the ability to do it. Very likely it may stretch you beyond what you have done before. He wants you to grow. In Christ we are bigger. Whatever lies before you, God put it there. You can move mountains. Do not measure what you should do by your gift, measure the gift by what you should do. It will match. God is a God specializing in the impossible, and thinks only in terms of the impossible. He wants this fact to show in the lives of those who belong to Him. He commands the impossible, and then makes it possible, to his glory. Perhaps you wonder why God should want us to do anything at all when he has all the power. It is because He loves us, and likes to share his pleasures and joys with us. That is his grand design, planned that way. You may feel you are a very small instrument, but each one is vital in the full orchestrated effort. The Lord of all the earth has big things in mind, but they call for millions of helpers with varied gifts and capabilities. We are 'vessels' so that the power may be of God and not of us,' as Paul said in 2 Corinthians 4: 7. 'I have learned that I can do all things through Christ who strengthens me' (Philippians 4: 13). And so can you, in the name of Jesus." (Reinhard Bonnke)

"Where you are, or where you start from does not limit you or determine where you can reach or what you can achieve. Many great names in history (including the Master Jesus!) started humbly; in fact, under circumstances that were almost impossible for success. Bill Gates of Microsoft and Steve Jobs of Apple, for example, did not complete a university education but they saw themselves differently! With your own background, circumstances, opportunities, and more exposure to civilization, you have the potential to achieve more than they did. Imagine and create new opportunities in your mind, in the spiritual, and they will be created and manifested in the physical". Rosicrucian monograph.

"All that we are is the result of what we have thought. The mind is everything. What we think, we become" (Gautama Buddha).

Imagine a better and greater you, see a better and greater family and a better and greater nation. It is only then that we can transform, rebuild, and re-create ourselves, our families, our nations, and our world.

God commanded Man to go into the world and multiply and have dominion over all he created. How do you multiply, bear fruit, create and build? How do you have dominion if you continue to see yourself as slave, as the crumb of society, as a poor participant in the affairs of the nation? See yourself as prosperous, rich, healthy, happy, multiplying your talents and having dominion over the affairs of your life and your environment.

You can only get as far as the limits you have in your imagination. So reach out and increase. You are meant to soar high in the sky as an eagle and not crawl as a worm on the ground. Let your imagination be positive and real. Even when things go in the opposite direction to your dream, be patient. Dreams will always come to pass, to manifest if you imagine them so.

You may seem crazy, but you need to be crazy to do a great thing! Very strong desires fire our vision and imagination. With determination and positive action we realize positive results and positive manifestation, or what might be called miracle, invention and discovery. No miracle happens without a strong desire!

To change your situation, change your imagination; change your picture of yourself. Your mind is like the film in a camera. As it is exposed to light, a picture is captured there. That picture in your mind (your imagination) is what is printed out and enlarged as reality in your life. Therefore, when you pray let what you ask for match the picture in your imagination. If there is disparity or conflict, then your desires or wishes do not materialize.

Create and invent your future. We human beings are creatures of habit. The greatest battle we have to fight is the internal one. Change your habits and you will change your life. Form the habit to give out of yourself, of your possessions and meet other people's needs. Sow seeds of good thoughts and visualize your harvest. Life is a journey and not a station! Once you make it a station, a final bus stop, you get into failure and frustration. So move to a higher level every day.

As a leader, use your imagination to create a new level for yourself, for your family, your organization, your state, your nation and for the whole world. Keep on working at being a great success! May the Lord bless all our efforts to create a better future.

Conclusion: impossibility is not a heavenly vocabulary word, because there is no impossibility found in God. And if we carry his glory inside of us, there shouldn't be any impossibility found in us.

You have all it takes to make the impossible possible. So, when they tell you it is impossible, there are many possibilities around. Just take the step of faith, be optimistic, and believe God.

Seeds of Self-Fulfilment

The kind of body you have, the kind of home you live in, the type of work you do, the kind of people you meet, are all conditioned by and correspond to the images in your mind. As there can be no plant without a seed, so the circumstances in your life spring from the hidden seeds of your thought. Every one of your actions is always preceded by thought.

Action then could be thought of as the flowering of thought; joy and suffering are its fruits. So when choosing the fruits of your life ..., a healthy body, a satisfactory job, friends and opportunities ..., you must first plant the seed of thought and supply yourself with the proper image in your mind before the thing will be manifested in your life.

Without the mental image within, you cannot have the material expression without ... ; "as within, so without."

There are probably things you would like to change or eliminate in your life, and let's face it, we all have them!

Perhaps you would love to change some habits. If you erase the mental image from your mind, that is, stop thinking about the unwanted condition, you will have taken the first step towards removing it from your life. The secret of successful living is to build up or visualize the mental image you want, whilst at the same time getting rid of the mental image you don't want. How do you do this? By choosing the thoughts you allow your mind to dwell upon.

Thoughts by nature externalize. You've heard the old saying "like attracts like …," well you tend to attract to yourself and to become attracted to people, circumstances and situations that are similar to the images you hold in your thoughts. If you think about happiness, you'll attract happiness into your life. But it's impossible to be successful and happy while you think about and hold an image in your mind of failure and sadness.

Remember, the type of thought you concentrate on and hold in your mind will reproduce itself in your outer world: for as within, so without.

Most people want to become happy, healthy and prosperous. But do you hold that image in your mind?

Gird Your Mind

The thought seed, or the creative idea, must be nourished and kept alive through its gestation period just as with any other life form. An egg for instance, has within it a tiny seed capable of becoming a chicken. But before you can see the material manifestation, namely the chicken, the mother hen must have enough interest during the three-week gestation period to nourish the egg by keeping it warm with her body, turning it in various positions with the expectation of seeing a chick. If the hen loses interest and fails to sit on the egg, the chick will be stillborn. The manifestation then is a rotten egg. It's the same with your thoughts and ideas.

Lose interest and fail to act, and your idea becomes the equivalent of a rotten egg.

If you want to be successful, concentrate your thoughts on things such as love, wisdom, joy and beauty, and nourish your thoughts and ideas throughout the gestation period. Your mind must be open and receptive, and intuitively you'll be directed toward your highest good by the Cosmic Energy within. Just as the hen acts intuitively in changing an egg into a chicken, you can act intuitively to change your idea into its material manifestation.

Think about a camera! In a camera there is of course no question of pressure. The secret lies in focus and depth of field. If you want to photograph an object, you focus your camera lens quietly and steadily on the object and calmly select your depth of focus. You don't press violently against the lens of the camera and you don't move the camera from one item to another, moment by moment.

If you did, you would end up with a blur. The same is true with the picture you are developing in your mind when you don't keep your thoughts concentrated for any length of time. In attempting to concentrate, some people think health for a few minutes and then wander off to thoughts of ill health or fear. They think prosperity a while, and then without knowing even, start worrying about their debts and how they're going to pay their bills. They think about bodily perfection and then think about old age, aches and pains. No wonder they produce a blurred image?

The thoughts must be positive, constructive, harmonious and about your desire.

By thinking quietly and without effort you'll attain the mental image of all-round success. When you have an image of success in your mind, success will follow in your outer experiences in the form of a healthier physical body, happier relationships, more productive work and spiritual development at its peak for as within, so without.

Your true thoughts and beliefs are projected in your daily experiences, and correspond with the circumstances in your life. True activity always comes from within and is manifested outward. False activity tries to come from outward to inward. As with the seed and the egg I spoke about earlier, growth comes from within.

The seed and the egg contain everything necessary to create life in a visible form. The tiny mustard seed, so small you can't see it once you place it in the soil, will burst forth from within and produce a plant two feet tall. If you do a project because you've been inspired from within and you act on that inspiration, that's a true action and you are working from within outward. Your work is alive and will be productive. If you're working from outside inward, your work will not be productive; in fact it will fail.

Thoughts of fear, doubt and indecision crystallize into weak and irresolute habits, which solidify into failure. Impure thoughts of every kind …, thoughts of envy, jealousy, revenge, injustice or unfair criticism, crystallize into confusing habits which solidify into adverse circumstances. On the other hand, beautiful thoughts crystallize into habits of grace and kindness, which solidify into genuine, cheerful and pleasant circumstances. Pure thoughts of love, health and happiness crystallize into habits of temperance and self-control which solidify into circumstances of success and peace. Just as lovely, pleasing and enjoyable thoughts produce sweet positive results so do sour, disagreeable and offensive Thoughts result in sour unattractive and negative results. If you persist in a particular train of thought, whether good or bad, it cannot fail to produce its results in your character and in your world.

So look at yourself and your life. Are you pleased with what you see? If you want to improve your life, you must improve yourself. Begin by changing your thoughts, for much of the misfortune you encounter in life is as a result of your own inharmonious thoughts having led you to the circumstances that brought the misfortune about.

The peace and harmony in your life is a result of your own mental harmony within. You are meant to be a happy, healthy and prosperous person; and happiness, health and prosperity are the result of a harmonious adjustment of the inner with the outer: for as within, so without. Be and remain a free thinker, think for yourself and not according to what others think.

Rosicrucian heritage No:2- 2011 Mary Ann Fowler, SRC

Final Word

"However, as it is written: No eye has seen, no ear has heard, no mind has conceived what God has prepared for those who love Him" (1 Corinthians 2: 9 NIV).

Beloved, the Lord wants to do great and mighty things in your life and to empower you to do the same, but first you have to open up your spirit to receive him.

The greatest gift God has given to man is free will, which implies that he cannot force you to receive him. But it is important you do so, having come to an understanding of the mighty works you can do when you return his love by believing in his Son Jesus and accepting him and the life of prosperity and ease you can have here on earth.

The book of 1 John 4: 17 states that love is made perfect among us so that we will have boldness in the Day of Judgment, because, as he is, so are we in this world.

Wake up every morning with the mindset that as he is so are you in this world. Say to yourself that God is not a failure;

therefore, I will not fail, with an understanding of the fact that the Zoë life (the God kind of life) becomes infused in you when you become born again. Say to yourself, "I have the life of God in me; therefore, I can do all things." Therefore, you, as a believer, can transcend from the realm of impossibility to possibility by calling forth things that be not as though they were. First, you have to accept Christ as your Lord and personal saviour if you haven't, or rededicate yourself to him to have access to a full measure of his unmerited and uninterrupted grace.

The psalmist said in Psalm 119: 11 (KJV), "Thy word have I hid in my heart that I might not sin against thee." And verse 105 says, "Thy Word is a Lamp unto my feet and a light unto my path." It is the Word that shines and gives direction. Allow the Word to illuminate your path today, for the Word contains all you need to function on earth as a believer.

God bless you.

Prayer for Salvation

Father, I come to you today in the name of your Son, Jesus. I believe I have transgressed and come short of your glory in several ways. I believe your Son gave his life for me to cleanse me of my iniquities, so I accept him this day as my Lord and personal Saviour.

Give me the grace to live a sin free life and to serve you in the days of my youth and all the days of my life so I can be who you have called me to be. Fill me with the Holy Spirit, today, as I start my life afresh in you.

Amen.

References

"God's Purpose for Sex and Marriage." Reprinted with permission. Published by United Church of God, *an International Association.* © 2014 United Church of God. http://www.ucg.org/christian-living/gods-purpose-sex-and-marriage

http://churchandmission.org/possibilities.htm Rev Israel Olu Kristilere